The Polished Perspective

TAPPING INTO THE TRANSFORMATIVE POWER OF POLISH, POISE AND ETIQUETTE

NATASHA TUPPER

THE POLISHED PERSPECTIVE

Tapping Into The Transformative Power Of Polish, Poise And Etiquette

By

Natasha Tupper

TABLE OF CONTENTS

INTRODUCTION

Congratulations on taking a major step in supercharging your life by turning on the lens of the Polished Perspective and tapping into the transformative power of polish, poise and etiquette.

Let's face it, it's not easy seeing others advance while you feel stuck. Stuck in your career, stuck in your way of thinking, stuck in self sabotage and stuck in unhealthy thoughts about yourself. The Polished Perspective will undoubtedly supercharge your life and empower you to once and for all change YOUR world from the inside out. Trust me, living out your divine purpose is far greater than waking, cooking, cleaning, working, sleeping and waking again to do it all again…the same way.

This book will transform your current life into the full and vibrant life that you were meant to have. Believe it or not, polish, poise, grace, etiquette and manners can open doors that have been traditionally closed for you. Conversely, the lack of these precious tools will always close the doors that you so deeply desire to have open. Apply these simple tips, tricks and secrets and watch how you transform into your true, vibrant, polished self.

Being a low-income kid from Detroit, I was not introduced to etiquette. Frankly, the lack of basic etiquette skills caused me to be at an even further disadvantage than my neighborhood, poverty, absent father and low self-esteem. I remember being embarrassed about not knowing which fork to use when I was invited out to dinner by the kind people at the church I attended with a neighbor. I was so excited to be a part of a group of people that were smart and kind and most importantly, led me to realize the love and reconciliatory nature of Christ. I vowed to sharpen my social intellect and learn more about etiquette, simply to fit in. I had no idea that it would morph into my life's work as a mentor, coach and author on the subject matter. The work that I vowed to do has helped countless girls and women empower themselves and amplify their personal lives and careers by walking in a more polished version of themselves. There's something to be said about a woman that goes the extra mile and looks great doing it!

Not only have I used these tips, tricks and secrets daily to attain personal and business success, those who've taken my courses and applied the wisdom from my books have actualized a higher level of success and self-awareness and they ultimately go on to impact in the world exponentially. They've been able to pass these tips, tricks and secrets down to their children, grandchildren and even in their business culture, providing generational and residual impact. In business, they've seen their sales skyrocket.

The sooner you read, digest and apply these tips, tricks and secrets the sooner you can meet your new polished self and change your world…from the inside out.

Step One: Show Up Every Day...Camera Ready

One of the simplest and most important things a woman can do from the polished perspective is literally show up every day. Show up for yourself first, then be sure to show up for others. And don't just show up like a 10th grader who's forced by law and parents to go to school but show up because your presence enhances everything. Show up because you desire to be there, there for yourself and for others. Don't just show up, SHOW UP! Grab your best suit, your finest pumps and your most distinguished handbag. Enhance your face with makeup (just a little...or a lot) and pay attention to your hair and your well-groomed nails. You are a well, a source of inspiration, grace, polish and poise. The world is better, because you're here.

THE POLISHED WOMAN KNOWS HER WORTH AND SHOWS UP EVERY DAY...CAMERA READY

Step Two: Activate HOPE (Help One Person Everyday)

I was recently enrolled in an online course that empowers CEO's to amplify their messaging. One of my favorite takeaways was the HOPE paradigm. It simply reminds those who are in areas of influence to Help One Person Everyday (HOPE).

Essentially, the polished perspective would have you to ask this one question at the end of every day. "Did I Add Value to Someone's Life Today". If your answer is no, then you're not using your influence properly.

Step Three: Throw Yourself A Daily Parade Of Etiquette

Being polished is not reserved for special occasions! A lady is always polished. It has been said that what you practice becomes habit. Business and personal success is nothing more than the accumulation of great habits practiced every day.

The polished perspective is one that urges influential women to shine daily. I invite you to throw yourself a daily parade of etiquette. Dine like there's a Maître D, even if you're at home. Use your manners. Pretend that you're dining with a queen, because one day that could very well be your reality. Simply put, shine forth every day!

Step Four: PREpare…Today's Preparations Were Made Yesterday

I can recall a recent local news interview that I was blessed to land. I spent 2 days prior to the interview rehearsing my messaging, pulling out my interview outfit and preparing my in- home virtual interview space. Everything that you plan to do well requires thoughtful PREparation.

The polished perspective knows that today's successes are based upon yesterday's preparation. Tweak the messaging, lay out the attire, study, practice and create impact BEFORE the bell rings.

Step Five: Keep It Classy…Always

I have four eyes…I wear glasses. I've noticed a hiatus of class, polish and poise in women. Quite frankly it doesn't take four eyes to see it…I'm sure we've all seen it at one point or another. We've seen it in others and have even seen it in ourselves on occasion. It happens! Sophistication is on the decline and we're all suffering the effects.

Never mind what the masses are doing! Be different. Be peculiar. Be discerning. Stand out! Keep it refined and chic…Always. Let's bring polished back!

Step Six: Resist Fleeting Trends

Sometimes trends can be so cool, different and …trendsetting! Here's the thing though, you never really see polished women being overtaken with the latest trends. Trends are just that, they're trendy…they come and go. Some trends are good and some not so good. Remember zoot suits? Remember M.C. Hammer pants? Remember Applebottom jeans? Remember long coffin shaped fake nails?   Just don't…per the polished perspective.

The sophisticated woman's wardrobe should be 80% classic while saving a small 20% for well-designed and flattering trendy garments. Classy doesn't need trendy!

Step Seven: Pocketbook Faith

One thing that every woman that resides within the polished perspective shares is a sense of faith. Faith in something, even if it's a simple faith in herself. I personally place every ounce of faith in God. He's given me the creativity and ability to reach the masses with a message of faith and grit, humbleness and genius, reconciliation and refinement!

The polished woman
never leaves home without
her faith. Be sure to toss it in
that fabulous handbag along
with your sunglasses, lip
gloss, phone, keys, money
and mints. Faith…never
leave home without it.

Step Eight: Polished Pennies

The polished perspective concentrates on polish and refinement in every area of our lives. Our money is not exempt. Let your pennies be well polished! Simply put, a polished woman is a good steward of her finances.

Watch your dollar as closely as you watch your wit, wardrobe and flatware placement. The polished woman can attract, generate, retain, give away and pass down wealth!

STEP NINE: IMPACT AND EMPOWER HER

As we near the end of this short and highly impactful work, I want to leave you with some marching orders as you step out and into your highly polished self. Always think beyond yourself. While my personal journey started with self-refinement, it continues with a nationwide movement to ensure that girls and women are equipped and empowered to activate their most polished selves and as a result attract and retain success.

"If you have knowledge,
let others light their candles in
it".

~Margaret Fuller~

Step Ten: Rehearse Your Whoa Moments Daily

Sometimes we can forget how wildly amazing we really are. I remember being prompted to write down my top 10 amazing moments (the instructors called it something a little more colorful, but polished women don't swear honey!). As I sat in my well designed egg chair with pen in hand, I struggled to come up with the first thing. Then it dawned on me…everything that I'd been blessed to overcome, achieve, power and lament through.

The polished perspective causes us to look over our lives and rehearse our most amazing moments on a daily basis. This generates instant gratitude, forecasts future accomplishments and reminds the universe of who you are!

BONUS

Our time together has been absolutely amazing and beautiful. Before I send you back out into the world with your newly acquired polished perspective, allow me to share a few bonus nuggets for the polished woman, because after all, the polished woman always go above and beyond when it comes to adding value.

The very first and last thing you should do every day is tap into and accelerate your gratitude. It puts everything into perspective and makes room for future gratitude moments. Every day find a way to give back. Giving back doesn't always mean giving money, though the polished woman is a philanthropist in her own right. Sometimes giving back is encouraging those in need. Sometimes giving back is sowing into the lives of others with your expertise. Sometimes giving back is writing a check to your favorite local non-profit. Big box non-profits normally have far greater capacity than local, grass roots nonprofit organizations, so keep that in mind when you give. Let's shoot for the greater impact.

Lend your voice to the voiceless. Amplify the voices of those who go unheard. Whatever your cause is, be loud and proud about it. Bring awareness to those who need to build capacity and realize change and commitment.

Lastly, rest and practice self-care daily. While the polished woman is well groomed, that's not what I'm referring to. Self-care is greater than the fabulous blowout and shellac manicure. Rest well and take moments alone to yourself daily. Sit quietly, pray, think, meditate, breath deeply and chase your God given genius. It'll supercharge and prepare you to continue to provide added value to everyone that you come across.

ABOUT THE AUTHOR

When it comes to showing girls and women how to gain limitless success by boosting their confidence and mastering door-opening etiquette skills and attention-grabbing poise, no one does it better than Natasha Christina Tupper, founder of The Polished Institute.

Known as the "Transformer of Women," Natasha has turned the idea of "being polished" into a successful strategy that empowers women and girls to unleash their inner confidence and recognize the value they bring to the table, all while encouraging others to do the same.

Having been featured on *CBS News, ABC, NBC* and *FOX,* Natasha is a mentor and coach on a mission to teach women and girls how to tap into their power and take their rightful place in "running their world."

As the host of *The Polished Perspective* podcast and the International #1 Bestselling Author of three books on the subject matter, she is relentless in her quest to educate females about how being polished and poised can unlock doors that have traditionally been closed for women. And with Natasha's guidance, everyday women gain the know-how to turn their dreams into a reality as they actualize tremendous success by displaying the polish, poise and grace that makes them stand out unforgettably.

When she's not teaching poise and etiquette to women-based audiences worldwide, Natasha is teaching her 10-year-old daughter how to shatter glass ceilings and soar above the limits that society sets for women and girls.

Natasha speaks on topics ranging from "the lost art of being a lady" to the life- changing effect of mastering poise, and she has undoubtedly made it her life's work to empower women to walk in their destiny. Find out more about Natasha and The Polished Institute at www.thepolishedinstitute.com.